WHY ME, LORD?

WHY ME, LORD?

Meaning and Comfort in Times of Trouble

CARL W. BERNER

AUGSBURG PUBLISHING HOUSE
Minneapolis, Minnesota

To my mother

Her valiant faith
is a shining light
to her children.

WHY ME, LORD?

Copyright © 1973 Augsburg Publishing House

Library of Congress Catalog Card No. 73-78267

International Standard Book No. 0-8066-1331-9

Scripture quotations unless otherwise noted are from the King
James Version. Quotations from the Revised Standard Version
(RSV), copyright 1946 and 1952 by the Division of Christian
Education of the National Council of Churches; from *The New
English Bible* (NEB) copyright 1961 by Oxford University
Press; from *The New Testament in Modern English* (Phillips)
copyright 1958 by J. B. Phillips; from *The Living Bible* (LB)
copyright 1971 by Tyndale House Publishers; and from *The
Jerusalem Bible* (JB) copyright 1966 by Darton, Longman &
Todd, Ltd. and Doubleday & Company, Inc. are used by
permission.

MANUFACTURED IN THE UNITED STATES OF AMERICA

Contents

Triumph Over Trouble

Hazel Garey is the proof. God taught her how to triumph over trouble. She went home after sixteen operations—serious ones. In her latest one they took off her second leg.

"Hazel," I said, "God has taken you into a special school. What have you learned?"

Her face shone. "I learned to have joy and confidence in God's will. My life centers on one thing now: follow his wisdom. It's greater than mine; and his love is deeper. I am content in his hands. They are the safest and best in the world." There's no question about it. Hazel Garey is a Christian who is now very close to God. Her suffering did it.

John Engel is different. He didn't even bother

to ask God for help when trouble came. He thought only of himself and his problem—not about God's plan. When the doctor said, "John, you have cancer," he lost about 80% of his faith. He was shocked. He spun his emotional wheels. His lament: "I just can't believe it. I saw it happen to others but never dreamed it would happen to me. My life has turned to ashes. What's the use?"

God offers a message to his suffering followers. In effect, it reads like this:

My dear sons and daughters:

I am inviting you to an orientation course. It's called "How to Triumph Over Trouble." Every person born into the world is a bundle of trouble. And trouble compounds.

Who's the arch trouble-maker? It's Satan. He and trouble are buddies. They work together hand and glove: like con men and gangsters. His purpose is to drive you into the ground; but my purpose is to elevate. Satan wants the worst; I want the best. He wants to make you stumble; I want to make you soar heavenward. He sends pain to injure; I use it to heal.

One thing Satan cannot do. He can't call on me for help. But you can. Will you let me help you? I will show you how to turn pain into gain, grief into growth, crosses into crowns, and adversity into prosperity.

In short, by your faith, sons and daughters, you can gain a clear-cut victory over Satan, over the world, *and over suffering and pain* through me, your heavenly Father.

By suffering, Jesus gained the victory. Satan tried to throw him off course. But Jesus stood firm. He had a vision of "the joy that lay ahead of him." The joy of victory. The joy of having us at his side. For this he endured all the shame and pain.

God raised him to heights of glory. He will do the same for us.

1.

Lord,
How Could
You?

"Man is born to trouble as the sparks fly upward" (Job 5:7).

Trouble is everywhere. You will find it in every shepherd's hut in the Alps or every mansion in Palm Springs.

Trouble is here because this is a broken world. It will stay that way until God puts the pieces together again and builds a new one. He promised he would, along with a new heaven.

My Christian parents called this world a vale of tears. I hated that kill-joy expression. I was having a lot of fun and couldn't understand how anyone saw drear instead of cheer. But

13

my parents were right. I soon learned this world *is* a vale of tears. Anguish abounds, as do famines, wars, sickness, accidents, tidal waves, earthquakes, avalanches, cave-ins, tornados and typhoons. The daily headlines scream heartbreak: "Jet-liner Crashes—86 Dead"; or "Earthquake Levels 40 Towns—Death Toll Mounts"; or "Rhodesia Mine Disaster Kills 440"; or "Capitol of Nicaragua Devastated"; or "Volcano Splits Island off Iceland—5,000 Homeless." And so on.

Our Turn Will Come

When your turn comes, how will you respond? Will suffering and pain send you into a tizzy? Will it sweep you off your feet? Will it make you bitter or better? When God lets life slap you down, will you learn his purpose and accept it?

These are important questions. They should be settled before trouble-tremors hit. But even when trouble is expected, it always comes as a surprise. There's no notice. It strikes sharply and suddenly. And it stabs at the center of our emotions. We are in danger of being swept into a riptide of despair. Lifeguards say you can't fight a riptide and win. You have to ride it out to safe waters.

That's what Myrus Knutson, a friend of mine did. He met the blow with fortitude. The "terminal cancer" diagnosis of three doctors hit him hard, but he refused to go down. He stood firm in faith: "I remember the first thoughts that came to me when the doctors broke the news," he said. "At once I felt myself in God's hands. He had given me a rich and beautiful life. He didn't owe me even a minute more. I felt no resentment or rebellion. I felt myself lifted by the Holy Spirit into a new kind of world."

This man faced his problem. But not alone. The first thing he did was to bring God into it. His faith, and the faith of his praying friends, was the secret of complete recovery. The doctors couldn't believe what they saw, and they couldn't understand what happened. But Pastor Knutson and his friends knew. And they gave God all the glory.

When Trouble Hits

The first thing to do is to assert an action of faith. Find your strength in the Lord. Grasp the promise of his presence. That will be enough for the moment. When trouble is there he is there. "Know that I am with you always," Jesus said (Matt. 28:20, JB).

That promise is the first one to reach for in your spiritual first-aid kit. No matter what the trouble is, you are not facing it alone. He is there to help you. Say it over and over again, "I will fear no evil for thou art with me." Evil forces are all around. But with us there is One more powerful than all the legions of evil put together. Someone is present with us, Someone strong and resourceful, Someone who is for us and not against us.

Awareness of God's presence will steady us in the initial attack of trouble. This will keep us firm on the inside while emotions simmer down.

Grasp His Hand

Tribulations never come alone. God always comes with them. He has his hands in them. And those hands are strong and trustworthy. They will never let go. "None shall be able to pluck them out of my hands," he promised (John 8:28). The only thing we need to fear is that in a moment of weakness we may pull our hand out of his. He won't pull his hands out of ours. In every trouble he holds out his hand and whispers, "Friend, take hold and hang on. Together we'll make it."

"Those who look to the Lord will win new strength . . . they will march on and never grow faint" (Isa. 40:31 NEB).

Where Does All the Trouble Come From?

"Our fight is not against human foes, but against cosmic powers . . . against the super-human forces of evil" (Eph. 6:12 NEB).

Superhuman forces of evil have twisted the heart out of shape and the world out of order.

Evil exists not just on the fringes of man's life but at the very core. "The whole head is sick and the whole heart faint," says Isaiah (1:5, 6). "From the sole of the foot even unto the head there is no soundness in it."

Nathaniel Hawthorne tells of a place where zealous reformers succeeded after long effort to close all dance halls, taverns, gambling casinos, and race tracks. They looked at these as "the chief source of corruption" in their community. Now they saw a trouble-free life. The devil chuckled to himself: "There's one thing these do-gooders have overlooked. They have forgotten to tear out their own hearts."

The heart of man is the source of all ills that plague humanity: wars, famines, sickness, sufferings, accidents, death. "From whence come wars and fightings among you?" asks James. "Come they not hence even of your lusts that war in your members?" (James 4:1).

The evil power is seen in convulsions of nature: earthquakes, tidal waves, typhoons, tornados, hurricanes, droughts, floods. "The whole created universe," Paul says, "groans in all its parts as if in the pangs of childbirth" (Rom. 8:22 NEB).

Evil Not from God

Where did all the evil come from? Who is responsible? God created the world in flawless perfection. Who upset the apple cart?

Some put the blame on God. He could have prevented it, they say. Archibald MacLeish comes to a grim conclusion: "If God is God he is not good; if God is good he is not God." Bible believers reject a slick expression like that. There's no question about God's faultless integrity.

18

God's Word pinpoints the source of evil: "An enemy hath done this," it says. "The devil," said Christ, "is a murderer from the beginning." He is "the father of lies," and this arch-foe of God and man is responsible for all evil.

Evil was conceived not on earth but in the world of spirit-persons. Though humans fell into sin, they did not invent sin. Man was sin's victim, not its designer. This explains why God provides redemption for mankind, not for the devil and the evil angels. The ones "Who kept not their first estate," God has "reserved in everlasting chains under darkness unto the judgment of the great day" (Jude 6).

Some think Christians are simpleminded for believing in a personal devil. Unbelievers are too self-sufficient for that. But the burden of the proof is on them. If there is no devil, who is keeping up his work? "Don't tell me there is no devil," Billy Sunday stated. "In the first place the Bible declares that there is a devil, and secondly, I have done business with him."

How Did the Devil Become the Devil?

To noble beings created in his image God gave the power of free choice. These were not

19

robots, machines that go through their paces. For intelligent dialog and fellowship God created spirit-persons and earth-persons capable of ethical conversation. That required freedom of decision. But freedom to choose the right includes freedom to choose the wrong. Once he gave man free choice, God could not retract or restrict that choice. Free choice would no longer have been free. Man would have been a wind-up toy manipulated by a God who likes to play games.

It was Lucifer, the most clever of all angels, who made the fateful choice for evil. With him stood a great host of angel-persons who joined in his conspiracy. In the Apocalypse the dragon is seen sweeping one-third of the stars out of heaven with his tail. Some interpret this to mean that one-third of the angels followed Satan's plot to overthrow God.

Lucifer's abilities were superlative. His very name suggests that he was a bearer of light. He had primacy over the angel-host whose number was "ten thousand times ten thousand" (Dan. 7:10). He was supreme master of angels, archangels, cherubim, seraphim, thrones, dominions, principalities, powers: splendid orders God created for his glory and the good of man.

A dramatic passage in Isaiah describes the pattern of Satan's rise and fall. "Thou hast said in thy heart, I will exalt my throne above the stars of God . . . I will be like the most high" (Isa. 14:13-14). God's judgment was prompt: "Thou shalt be brought down to hell."

A Demon of Frightful Power

Dethroned, disgraced, destined for destruction, the loathsome potentate of perversion was obsessed with fiendish rage to destroy everyone and everything that is of God.

Satan is frightfully powerful and resourceful. The first chapters of the book of Job show that he can control the weather, our health, the lives of our children, the thoughts of our friends. Sometimes we murmur against God for misfortunes and disasters for which Satan is to blame. So powerful and intelligent is this old evil foe that, in the perversion of his pristine perfection, he challenges even God's best efforts. He is capable of entering our minds, implanting evil thoughts in our heads. His disguises are good foolers and many: an angel of light, a wolf in sheep's clothing, a roaring lion. Sometimes he can make use of our friends for

21

his nefarious ends. Our closest companions, even intimate members of our own family, can be his unwitting tools.

What God Has Done

God did not in icy justice reject man, who ignored his warning of Satan's trap. In tender mercy he stooped down to his fallen children. "I will put enmity between your despoilers and you," he promised in effect, "I will not let Satan ruin you altogether. I will be on your side. I will send the woman's seed to crush Satan's head" (Gen. 3:15).

God took his place on our side against our enemies. That shows the kind of God we have. A God who allows his children to fall into evil powers and makes no provision for their escape is not the true God but a monster of man's imagination. God expresses his case against man in terms of loving sympathy, though man may express his alleged case against God in terms of harsh anger.

To understand this better we may in imagination picture millions of people gathered on a vast plain before God's throne. All have a complaint against God for the evil and suffering he permitted in the world. How fortunate he is to live in heaven where there is no weeping, no fear, no pain, no hunger!

"What does God know about suffering?" asked a young woman who had endured beatings and torture in a concentration camp.

"What about this?" a father demanded as he pointed to his son in a wheelchair, a palsy victim from birth.

After much heated talking the multitude decided to choose leaders to present their case against God. People who had suffered most were chosen as leaders. There was an untouchable from India, a survivor of Hiroshima, a scarred inmate of a Siberian slave camp.

After consultation with each other they were ready to present their case. Their decision was that God, to prove his alleged love and sincerity, would have to endure what they themselves had endured.

He must live on earth as a man and suffer the same as they had.

He must be betrayed by his friends. He must face false charges, be tried before a prejudiced jury, and be sentenced by an unjust judge. He must know what it is to be all alone, completely abandoned by every living person. He must be tortured and he must die. He must die the most humiliating death in the company of common rogues.

Loud murmurs of approval went up from the great throng as each leader announced his portion of the sentence.

But when the last leader had finished pronouncing sentence, there followed a long silence. No one spoke a word. No one moved. For suddenly all knew — God had already served his sentence.

God did something about evil. He set up the cross, and he himself suffered and died there. In the cross God's goodness met earth's evil. There was evil at its worst and love at its best.

A world of evil was not God's idea in the first place. It is not his plan in the last place. The total destruction of Satan and evil is in God's blueprint for the future. Why the delay? Why doesn't he eradicate all this evil right now? Why does he continue to let man suffer? God explains: "It is not that the Lord is slow in fulfilling his promise, as some suppose, but that he is very patient with you, because it is not his will for any to be lost, but for all to come to repentance" (2 Peter 3:9 NEB).

The full cleansing and renewal of the earth

disabling muscular dystrophy, painful angina, seems a dubious kind of love. It grows more suspect when we see how people who don't love God seem to suffer less than those who do. Offhand, it doesn't seem right that a devout Christian is wracked with pain while an unbeliever goes untouched.

What God allows Satan to do to his children remains an enigma. Asaph, author of many psalms, almost lost his faith over it. This vexing, inscrutable mystery almost got the best of him. And he has a lot of company.

Fortunately, Asaph recorded his thoughts in Psalm 73 while he was going through the severe tests.

As his psalm opens, Asaph is seen tottering on the edge of despair. "My feet were almost gone," he said; "my steps had well nigh slipped . . . when I saw the prosperity of the wicked. . . . They have more than heart could wish." So cocky and smug in their imagined security were these worldlings that they even scoffed at God. "They set their mouth against the heavens, and their tongue walketh through the earth. . . . And they say, how doth God know? . . . These are the ungodly who prosper in the world."

Asaph felt that he was getting a raw deal: "Verily I have cleansed my heart in vain, for all the day long have I been plagued and chastened." The perfidious ones had everything a heart could wish. "They are not in trouble as other men; neither are they plagued like other men."

Finally light dawned in Asaph's spirit. He saw the problem from God's side. He realized where he had made his mistake. The blues he had been singing were out of tune with the melody God was playing. "My heart was grieved," he said, "I was pricked in my reins. So foolish was I and ignorant: I was as a beast before thee." Asaph had made the mistake of looking at only one side of the ledger. He should have known that God doesn't balance his books every day, but he will balance them eventually. After heart-searching before God in the sanctuary Asaph saw the final issues. "Then understood I their end," he said. "They are brought into desolation . . . they are utterly consumed with terrors."

Now a new insight flashed into Asaph's soul. Once again he saw himself in the light of God's care and love. His spirit now snuggled in the arms of God. "I am continually with thee," he said confidently. He realized anew to whom he belonged: "Whom have I in heaven but thee? and there is none on earth that I desire beside thee. My flesh and my heart faileth; but God is the strength of my heart and my portion for ever."

"My portion for ever." That's the secret of triumph over trouble. If God is our "portion for ever," we can be joyful. He is the very source and well-spring of joy. Joy in God outweighs all trouble.

Samuel Rutherford put it this way: "When we come to the other side of the water, we shall be forced to say, 'If God had done otherwise with me, I would never have come to this crown of glory.'"

There is joy even in pain and suffering when we know that God will make everything work together for our good.

This is what we have to remember:

God's chastenings are as much a part of his faithfulness as his blessings.

In God's plan cross-bearing and crown-wearing go together.

The love that chose us also chastens us. The love that purchased us also purifies us.

The love that delivers us from death also disciplines us to life.

The troubles God allows are a challenge to try the soul's strength on.

Crosses Come in Many Sizes

"If anyone wishes to be a follower of mine," Jesus said, "he must take up his cross and come with me" (Matt. 16:24 NEB).

The cross is a symbol of Christianity. We use it in a profuse variety of designs, colors, sizes, materials. Cross collectors say that there are hundreds of styles and types. The most popular designs are: the Latin cross, the Calvary cross, the Greek cross, the Celtic cross, the Maltese cross, and the Jerusalem cross.

The cross that burdens God's children also comes in a great variety of forms.

1. *Some crosses are hereditary.* Through our solidarity with Adam we face the common ills of humanity. Millions are born blind, deaf, dumb, and with other mental or physical defects. If at birth we escape major genealogical maladies, we are thankful. But we may not boast. Our cross will come in time.

2. *Some crosses are the direct action of Satan.* Paul regarded his thorn in the flesh as "the messenger of Satan to buffet me." God turned the tables on Satan's "messenger," pressing him into his own service. He used the "thorn" to keep Paul humble. Paul understood God's purpose. "The thorn was given me," he said, "lest I be puffed up beyond measure by the abundance of revelations I received."

Jesus traced illness to Satan's power. When an indignant synagogue ruler censured him for healing a crippled woman on the Sabbath, Jesus answered: "Ought not this woman, being a daughter of Abraham, whom Satan hath bound, lo these eighteen years be loosed from this bond on the Sabbath day?" (Luke 13:16).

3. *Some crosses are biological.* Any one of hundreds of virulent germs can enter the body to bring sickness and pain. Cells go astray to create a malignancy. Glandular disfunctions throw the metabolism off course. The bloodstream is poisoned. The respiratory system fails. The nerves go on a rampage. Calcium deposits bring on arthritis.

This is the way it is in life. A child succumbs to leukemia. A strong, virile man, is struck down in the prime of life by a fatal blood disease. A young husband and father dies of a blood clot after surgery. A brilliant executive is felled by a heart failure. A mother of four is snatched away by a massive stroke. We have proof that a foreign power has wrought havoc in God's once serene and perfect order.

4. *Some are sociological crosses.* The society in which we live is good at creating evil, but not controlling it. Here is Paul's description of people in their natural state: "They are filled with every kind of injustice, mischief, rapacity and malice; they are one mass of envy, murder, rivalry, treachery, and malevolence" (Rom. 1:29-30 NEB).

We know Paul is right. Not one of us can escape the hurt and anguish resulting from gossip, bad temper, malice, selfishness, vengefulness. A bleeding heart hurts as much as a bleeding body.

We live in a society that is sick with sin. The Psalms are right in their frequent reference to "enemies," the God-haters, the proud-walkers, the big-talkers, the evil-doers, the filth-peddlers, who are working for Satan, against God.

5. *Some crosses are self-imposed and psychological.* Through ignorance, excesses, or disregard of basic health rules people sponsor their own sorrow. They worry themselves sick. They work themselves to death. They smoke too much and bring on emphysema. They drink too much and destroy the cells of the liver. They take dangerous drugs and blow their minds.

Paul, an expert in human living, lists the works of the flesh: fornication, impurity, indecency, idolatry, quarrels, a contentious temper, envy, fits of rage, selfish ambitions, dissensions, jealousies, drinking bouts. (Gal. 5:20-21 NEB.) The works of the flesh are not only bad, they are bad for us. They throw the human personality into disruption. Psychology would say as loud an "Amen" to that as does the Christian faith. Paul also lists the fruits of the Spirit. They are love, joy, peace, patience, kindness, goodness, faithfulness, gentleness, self-control. The works of the Spirit are not only good, they are good for us. They bring on well-being in body and mind. A prolonged flow of happy feelings and good will does more to brace up the system for constructive work than any other influence.

6. *Some crosses are borne vicariously.* Sometimes the crosses we bear in empathy for others are the heaviest of all. The Gentile woman whose engaging faith prompted Jesus to say, "O woman, great is thy faith," is an example of this kind of grief. Her burden was in reality her daughter's burden. She cried, "Lord, help me," but it was the daughter, "tormented by a demon," who needed help. Jesus admired this woman's persistent faith and deep love. He granted her prayer. That day two crosses were lifted from burdened shoulders, and the heavier one may have belonged to the mother (Matt. 15:22-28).

Four men, suffering in another's suffering, lowered their friend through a roof into the presence of Jesus. When Jesus saw "their faith" he healed the man. Some of the most valiant cross-bearers are they who have learned to weep with those who weep. If we have a heart, we will have a cross. Vicarious crosses may be the heaviest of all crosses. Who can describe the anguish of parents when a tenderly loved daughter forsakes a Christian home and takes a dive into moral filth? Or the agony of parents who see their son hooked on dope? Who can remain untouched when a good neighbor, father of a large family, loses his health and his job? Or when an entire family is wiped out in a car accident? Unless we have hearts of stone we will suffer in another's pain.

7. *Some are Christian-witness crosses.*

A sure cross will follow a true witness. "If they have persecuted me, they will also persecute you," Jesus said, and millions have experienced the truth of that prediction. Jesus offered no easy way. He did not come to make life easy, but to make men great. "All that will live godly shall suffer persecution" (2 Tim. 3:12). Paul was so sure of "the offense of the cross" that he warned his converts, "We must through much tribulation enter into the kingdom of God" (Acts 14:22). New Christians are forewarned not to be "moved by these afflictions . . . for you know that we are appointed thereunto . . . We told you before that we should suffer tribulation" (1 Thess. 3:3-4).

Through the centuries there have been waves of persecutions of Christians. There may be an intermittent lull, but then there's a new outbreak. The day of persecutions is not past. Within the last fifty years many millions of Christians in Russia and satellite countries have been persecuted, imprisoned, or executed. The Christian church of China, once numbering two million members has virtually disappeared.

God's Cross Lightens Ours

God knows what his children are suffering. He went through all the suffering himself. He is with us and suffers with us in our suffering. He shows us the triumph that will follow our tears, the crown that will follow our cross. This is clear from the story of Stephen. While the stones were crushing his body God gave Stephen a vision of "the glory of God and Jesus standing on the right hand of God" (Acts 7:55). Every stone that bruised his body was a trumpet call that summoned his spirit into glory.

It was in the suffering of his Son that God drew closest to man. It is still in suffering that God comes nearest to his children. Our extremity is always his opportunity. In our suffering his heart goes out to us, his hand is extended to us, his Spirit upholds us, his heaven beckons us. This explains why the early Christians could march to their death as though they were going to a picnic. They were. They were reaching out for something better than what they were losing. Their gain outweighed their pain. Looking back, comparing the former agony with the present ecstasy, they are now saying: "We would do it over again. So great is our present glory that all the suffering isn't worthy to be compared with it."

Cross-Bearing Goes with the Christian Life

Satan is what he is, God is what he is, and we are what we are. This makes cross-bearing unavoidable. There is no life without a cross. Neither is there a cross apart from God's power to turn it into a crown. Jesus never spoke of his death apart from his victory over it. And Christians should never look at the present cross apart from the promised crown.

When missionary James Calvert went to the Fiji Islands he was told, "You will risk your life and the lives of those with you if you go to those savages." Calvert's magnificent reply was: "We died before we came here."

Even before it comes, our minds should be made up to accept the cross as an opportunity to win the crown. A cross rejected is Satan's instrument of torture. A cross thankfully accepted is Christ's gentle yoke of training for the great triumph.

After the tears of Gethsemane came the glory of Easter morning. That's the way it was for Christ, and that's the way it is for us. After the cross comes the crown.

OUR GETHSEMANE

Down shadowy lanes, across strange streams
    Bridged over by our broken dreams;
Behind the misty caps of years,
    Beyond the great salt fount of tears,
The garden lies. Strive as you may,
    You cannot miss it in your way.
All paths that have been, or shall be
    Pass somewhere through Gethsemane.

All those who journey, soon or late,
    Must pass within the garden's gate;
Must kneel alone in darkness there,
    And battle with some fierce despair.
God pity those who cannot say,
    "Not mine, but thine," who only pray,
"Let this cup pass," and cannot see
    The purpose is Gethsemane.

—ELLA WHEELER WILCOX

2.

Lord,
Why?
Why Me?

"I will climb my watchtower now, and wait to see what answer God will give" (Heb. 2:1 LB).

"Lord, why are you doing this to me?" That question may be the most common and recurrent in the world. It is as permanent and persistent as trouble itself.

The question is in order, if sincere. And that is a big "if."

There's an interesting little story behind the word *sincere*. It is a union of two Latin words, *sine* and *cera*, meaning without wax. These two words were commonly placed on pottery displayed in the Roman market. Unscrupulous merchants would mend broken pots with colored wax, hiding the break. Ethical merchants refused to do that. They advertised their merchandise *sine cera*. The word *sincere* means to be perfectly honest, without deceit or hypocrisy.

If we are perfectly sincere when we ask the question, "Lord, why are you doing this to me?" we will await his answer. Often we ask the question and then provide our own answer. This insincerity not only disrespects God but defeats his purpose. Moreover, it hurts us, because the answer we provide is usually wrong. This leaves us facing a critical problem while clinging to a faulty solution. Worst of all, we muff the opportunity of learning what the Lord is trying to teach us—how to turn pain into gain, trials into triumphs, agonies into ecstasies.

An Old Prophet Shows the Way

The prophet Habakkuk offers the classic example of a person who asked the right questions, got the right answers, and achieved the right growth.

As the book of Habakkuk opens, the prophet is seen in utter dejection. And for good reasons. Everything seems to be going wrong. Godless, derisive, haughty Chaldean war lords are crushing God's people.

"How can a good God allow this to happen?" the prophet asks. All around him he observes that "The wicked devoureth the man that is more righteous than he. . . . The wicked doth compass about the righteous" (Hab. 1:4, 13).

In the second episode of the book God answers the prophet. "Look," he says, "here's what will astonish you and stun you . . . it is I who am raising up the Chaldeans. I am the One who has raised up this evil power to crush you and bring you to your knees." The prophet is dazed: "True we have sinned," he admits, "but there are some righteous among us who have not bowed the knee to Baal. How can a righteous God treat people like fish caught in a net in which all perish regardless?" Hab. 1:14-16 LB).

In the third episode the prophet enters a place of retreat. "I will," he said, "take my position on the watchtower." He wanted God's answers to the questions that were tugging at his tormented spirit. Here he would pray down light for his darkness. In prayer he would not so much speak to God as listen to God. He already knew what he would say to God. What he did not know, and wanted to learn, was what God had to say to him.

God answered the prophet, as he always answers the questing soul. God revealed to him a flash of divine truth which deserves to be emblazoned on the billboards of the world. It was a great light which all the darkness in the world cannot extinguish. With fanfare God introduces the revelation: "Write down the vision," God said, "Inscribe it on tablets, ready for heralds to carry it with speed."

The momentous truth God revealed to the prophet was compressed in seven little words. Illuminating words they are, monumental words, words as valid today as then: "The just shall live by his faith."

Faith Achieves the Victory

"The just shall live by his faith." These seven words hold the key to victory. "This is the victory that overcometh the world," St. John wrote, "even our faith" (1 John 5:4).

Faith joins us to God, justifies us before God, places us under his care and in his keeping. To those who trust him God opens a door of escape from evil. St. Paul was sure of it, "The Lord shall deliver me from every evil work" (2 Tim. 4:18).

Believers are sure that God will deliver them from all evil, in his own day and way. That ringing assurance resounds throughout the word. "God is our shelter and refuge," David sang, "a timely help in trouble; so we are not afraid when the earth heaves and the mountains are hurled into the sea" (Psalm 46:1-2 NEB).

The believer cannot go down to defeat, because God whom he trusts cannot go down to defeat. Even when they die under the enemy's fire, they continue to live in the Father's family.

Habakkuk came down from his retreat a changed man: faith, joy, and hope displaced fear, despondency, and despair.

The Leap of Faith for Children of Faith

Martin Luther, a great man of faith, saw faith as a bold leap across a deep chasm. He recommended that we take the "leap of faith" knowing that "the everlasting arms will catch and hold us." Faith that trusts God only when everything goes right is really no faith at all.

But to trust God when everything seems to be going wrong, that is true faith.

David, in Psalm 56, gives us a beautiful example of such faith. He wrote that psalm when everything seemed to be going wrong. His troubles were a mile high: "Enemies persecute me . . . assailants harass me all day long . . . they dog my footsteps . . . they lie in wait for me" (Psalm 56:1-6 NEB). But David's faith was as tall as his troubles. "This I know," he said, "God is on my side." God was on his side. That's all he needed to know. No trouble can stand up against the power of God. God's resources are more than a match for the greatest troubles. "My enemies will turn back on the day I call upon God." David was sure of that. "In God I trust and shall not be afraid." And why not? He knew what God had done for him, "Thou hast rescued me from death to walk in thy presence, in the light of life" (Psalm 56:9-13 NEB). A God who went that far for him would go all the way with him.

Jesus Extolled Faith's Power

Jesus was always ecstatic when he found people with faith. He gloried in faith as a miner does when he discovers gold. It wasn't Jesus' custom to lavish praise upon people. But he did so whenever he found faith. When Jesus saw the Roman centurion's faith he "admired the man," the Scriptures say, and he said to the bystanders: "I tell you, nowhere, even in Israel, have I found faith like this" (Luke 7: 9-10 NEB).

He gloried in the faith of the Gentile mother who brought her daughter to him for healing, "Woman, what faith you have! Be it as you wish!" (Matt. 15:28 NEB).

Faith is the hand that lays hold on the mighty power of God. When faith fails help fails. This key truth we must learn if we want God to help us in time of need.

Nothing saddened Jesus more than the unwillingness of people to believe him. So great is the sin of unbelief that the Scriptures assert "Without faith it is impossible to please God" (Heb. 11:6). We cannot please God in anything when we do not believe that he is able to help in everything. What we reject, we do not receive; what we do not receive, we do not have. Refusing to accept in faith what God offers we forfeit the help he longs to give. Of one area where Jesus visited the Scriptures assert: "He did not many mighty works there because of their unbelief" (Matt. 13:58). When the disciples were unable to help a distressed father who brought his son to them for healing, Jesus explained, "Your faith is too small" (Matt. 17:20 NEB).

When All Looks Wrong, Keep Faith Strong

When a mad killer in Chicago beat eight nurses to death, a bitter relative asked a pastor: "Where was God when this happened?" She then answered her own question—humanly. "I'll tell you what I think," she said. "I think God is dead. He had a heart attack. He doesn't care about us."

Faith folded here, it seems. If this woman had faith, she abandoned it when it was most needed.

We can feel for this woman. Sometimes we find it hard to reconcile our grief and God's goodness. The two seem miles apart. "How can a good God," we ask, "let things get so bad?"

Job Learned the Hard Way

A lot of people have stubbed their toes on this mystery. One of these was ancient Job.

48

This man experienced pain and anguish almost beyond human endurance. He lost all his possessions, his ten children, his health, and for a time, his faith. His friends came to comfort him, but their words were as vinegar upon his wounds. They contended that Job must be guilty of some secret sin for which God was punishing him. If he would admit that sin, he would have help from God. "Miserable comforters," Job called them. Their words were hard blows upon an already crushed spirit. He couldn't buy their line of reasoning. To him it was both cruel and offensive. That he had failed he was willing to admit. But that God would arbitrarily make his children suffer as he had suffered didn't square with his idea of God.

God Offers Help

Now God himself steps in. He speaks to Job. He doesn't explain. Instead, he explodes: "Hast thou entered into the treasures of the snow?" God asks. "Hast thou given the horse strength and clothed his neck with thunder?"

God does not reveal his grand design. Instead, he reveals himself. He does not show theologically why things are as they are. He does not say why a good man suffers when the wicked thrive. He does not explain to Job why he had to go through this horrible experience. But he did give to Job what he needed most: not a homily, but a hand to hold. That steadied Job. Though still wobbly, his faith was gaining strength.

Job saw his big mistake. He was questioning the love and wisdom of God. And he was doing so simply because it was beyond his limited understanding. This was wrong. He had no right to do that. After all, the tenant has no right to order the landlord off the premises. The student has no right to throw out the teacher and take over the class. The defendant has no right to cast the judge out of the courtroom.

God Knows What He's Doing

No man has the right to demand that the infinite God explain, step by step, why he is doing what he is doing.

Light blazed into Job's soul. "I had heard of thee by the hearing of the ear, but now my eyes see thee," Job said. To know God as friend was more important than to understand all his mysteries. "I do not know," Job said in effect, "why God allows these tragedies to happen. What's more, I do not need to know. I'm satisfied that he knows what he is doing. That's good enough for me." No longer does Job distress himself because he does not understand all that God does. Instead he says: "Though he slay me yet will I trust in him" (Job 13:15). No longer does Job say, "God must be dead." There's a new song in his heart: "I know that my redeemer lives" (Job 19:25).

What we learn from Job is this: instead of seeing only what the trials and tears are doing *to* us, we should try to see what God is doing through them *for* us. God is drawing us to himself. The present agony of suffering is a prelude to the radiant ecstasy of life eternal. The trumpets are sounding from the other shore. They are summoning us to keep the faith, to have courage and to be constant. "The sufferings of this present time," they are saying, "are not worthy to be compared with the glory which shall be revealed in us" (Rom. 8:18).

3.

Lord,
What Do
You Want?

"You do not understand now what I am doing," Jesus said, *"but one day you will"* (John 13:7 NEB). "Lord, what do you want?" This is a must question for all who want to advance in the art of cross-bearing.

It is a question that pleases God. He will not fail to answer it. It shows a teachable spirit.

But the question comes hard. Few ask it. We want to work out the problem in our own way. Thus we defeat God's purpose and shut out God's help.

God is always working on us. He tries wooing us by goodness and generosity. Failing in that, he tries hardness and rebuke. "God uses both the apple and the rod in dealing with us," said Martin Luther. This interplay of kindness and severity is the main theme of Psalm 78.

God Tries Both Ways

First the psalm rehearses God's goodness and love: "What marvelous things God did. . . . He brought streams out of the rock. . . . He opened the doors of heaven, and rained down manna. . . . Man did eat angels' food: he sent them meat to the full."

How did God's children respond? "For all this they sinned still, and believed not his wondrous works. . . . They tempted and provoked the most high God. . . . They were turned aside like a deceitful bow."

What did God do now? "He was wroth. . . . He gave his people over to the sword. . . . He delivered his strength into captivity, and his glory into the enemy's hand."

Then what? "The Lord awaked as one out of his sleep . . . and smote his enemies." When blessings failed, God blasted, but it was all in love. In this way "He fed them according to the integrity of his heart; and guided them by the skilfulness of his hands."

When life collapses at our feet and the

foundations crash, God is trying to tell us: "You can't make it without me. Better reconstruct your life on pillars that hold!"

"Lord, what do you want?" God has in fact already answered that question. He has told us how to, and how not to, respond to trouble. We had better listen, lest God will have to say of us what he said of others: "My people would not hearken to my voice, and Israel would [have] none of me. So I gave them up to their own hearts' lust. . . . Oh that my people had hearkened unto me. . . . He should have fed them with the finest of the wheat and with honey out of the rock should I have satisfied thee" (Psalm 81:11, 12, 16).

A Dialog with God

GOD: I want you to learn my will when troubles come, and my purpose in allowing it. I don't want you to have trouble without getting any good from it. So don't be indifferent to it. Don't give it the brushoff as being "just one of those things." Don't be ashamed of it, fearing people will think you weak or guilty. Don't let it take a lot out of you without getting something into you.

My Resolution: The first thing I shall do when trouble comes is to ask: "Lord, what are you trying to tell me? I know you have something good in mind. Please show me what it is." You promised, "I will instruct thee and teach thee in the way thou shalt go" (Psalm 32:8). Lord, I'm listening.

God: I want you to trust me when trouble comes. I do not want you to worry. As a responsible person you need to show concern. But worry is an irresponsible way of doing so. The right way is to assert an action of faith. Worry is an action of doubt. No matter what the problem is, trust me. I can always find a way to help you, and I'm on your side against Satan, who is always trying to get you to worry.

My Resolution: I will meet every problem in the strength of faith. I will guard myself against worry. I know that faith always leads to victory. Worry always goes down to defeat.

To overcome worry we need to see its futility. Worry always worsens a problem, never helps it. It never does any good. It offends God. It lowers our capacity for constructive, intelligent solutions.

Worry never robs tomorrow of its sorrow; it always saps today of its strength. It is not only useless, it is injurious. It may not be the greatest sin, but it is certainly one of the most destructive. It stirs the emotions, tangles the nerves, wears down the mind, tires the body.

Sure Cure for Worry

These are the anti-worry prescriptions of the Good Physician:

1. It is God who gave you the primary gift, life itself. Ought you not then trust him for other gifts needful for life?

2. It is impossible to secure your future by worry. Then why rub yourself raw trying?

3. Consider how lavishly God adorns flowers, birds, fields. Does it not follow that he will provide for you, the crown of his creation?

4. God took care of your yesterdays. Can

you not trust him to take care of your tomorrows?

5. You have to depend on God for all things — air, water, food, sunshine, rain. Isn't it silly to pick out a few things to worry about?

Faith Not Fatalism

GOD: I want you to believe that there is a good reason and a loving concern in everything I allow in your life. I do not want you to hold any fatalistic views.

The creed of the fatalist, that fate, at any time, for no good reason, has power to plunge a person into disaster and doom, is both fearful and dreadful. The belief that God is an impersonal force, like a giant mechanical computer incapable of love and mercy, is unworthy of a child of God.

The corollary of fatalism is superstition— putting stock in astrological predictions, attaching meaning to a black cat crossing the street, associating evil omens with dreams. This too is a contradiction of Christian faith.

MY RESOLUTION: To me God will always be

the essence of wisdom and love. I know that I am not exempt from the anxieties of life, but I also know that nothing can strike me apart from the good and gracious will of my heavenly Father. I thank God that I am released from the fatalistic fear that all humanity is caught in a cosmic crushing machine which operates without rhyme or reason. I thank God for the buoyant confidence of my Christian faith which enables me to live each day without fear. I know that nothing can reach me before it passes him whom I love as my heavenly Father. And when in his wisdom and love he brings me to the shadowed path, I know that even there I shall find some lovely flowers that grow only in the shade.

Trust in the Midst of Trouble

Under trouble some turn away from God and miss the blessing. Others turn to God and receive the blessing.

With some faith falters and God is defeated; with others faith surges and doubt is defeated.

The ideal is to trust God so completely that

you confidently accept whatever he sends, however painful it may be or irrational it may seem.

William Tedford missed the ideal. He couldn't accept as right what appeared to be wrong. This young man's brother, now forty, has been a spastic since he was five years old. His hands and legs are twisted and locked around his deformed body. The needed care has made the mother a virtual slave. Sympathy for his brother and mother, plus a feeling of helplessness in the face of this vexing problem has catapulted this man into a state of resentment. "Why isn't God doing something about this?" he asks indignantly. "I have looked at this problem from every angle," he sighs, "and I can't see any possible good in what God is allowing."

If this young man were not so obviously honest and sincere, we could write him off as a contentious, faithless individual. The world is full of petulant people who downgrade God when he allows trouble but never have a good word for him when all goes well.

Our young man wants to love and serve God. But events have driven him to the edge of despair. What shall we say to him? Shall we say: "William, you're questioning God but providing your own answers." Or, "William, you have no right to expect God to explain what he does." We admit that we cannot with our own reason or strength maintain trust in God when what he allows seems to have no redeeming quality. For this we need the Holy Spirit. He gives us faith to bank on God's love no matter what happens. He gives us power to trust God's wisdom even when his actions seem outrageous.

Our disturbed young man is missing an opportunity to trust God when everything looks wrong. Genuine trust, the kind that God wants, enables a man to say: "What I see seems all wrong, but what I believe makes it all right."

GOD: I want you to believe that I have a good purpose in all that I allow to happen. I do not want you to resent my way when it seems wrong. It still is right.

MY RESOLUTION: I will trust God's wisdom even when it doesn't agree with mine. His is higher and better. Just because I can't see what he is doing doesn't mean that he doesn't know what he is doing.

I will not scream and sulk at God when I can't understand his ways. I prefer to charge myself with ignorance rather than to charge God with unfairness.

I can see only a tiny part of God's total plan. His ways may not look good to me, but I know that they are good "because he is good and his mercy endureth forever." He has promised to make all things work together for good. I know "The Word of the Lord holds true" (Psalm 34:3 NEB).

Profit from Sickness?

Sickness is expensive. The economic setback may last for years. Often there is more than financial loss. There is pain, anguish, disruption of family life.

When we are sick, others profit—doctors, druggists, nurses, hospitals. Should we be the only ones to lose?

On the debit side sickness adds up to a big fat loss. What about the credit side? What are the gains? Do they match the losses? Are they worth the price? Whatever the cost, illness is a big bargain if it leads to wholeness of body, soul, and spirit. And that is what God wants. He sends pain for gain, and he wants the gains to outweigh the losses.

Walter Wessels, my doctor and friend for many years, told me of an experience in his life that led to a priceless discovery. Here's the way he put it: "When I was 32 I had a stomach ulcer that taught me a lesson I really needed. It led me to take stock of myself, to use good sense in eating, to regard work a privilege, to develop a joyful disposition." Reflecting upon his 54 years of productive activity the doctor said: "It was the ulcer that did it. That helped me to find the formula that served me well the rest of my life."

Albert Wunrow, made a similar discovery on the spiritual side. Perhaps the greatest day in his life came when he turned a corner and bumped into God. "The serious sickness I went through," he said, "was one of the best things that ever happened to me. When God put me on my back I learned to look up as never before. I have come out of this experience with a deeper faith, a truer view of life, a stronger grip on heaven."

Make Your Sickbed an Altar

Sickness-time is good investment-time. A Christian nurse helped a patient to a U-turn of attitude—from boredom and restlessness to a lovely, spirit-lifting ministry of achievement. She suggested that the patient use her hand as a pattern for a prayer program. She explained: "Let your thumb, which is nearest you, remind you to pray for those nearest and dearest to you —your spouse, father, mother, son, daughter, brother, sister, uncle, aunt. The index finger is known as the teacher's finger. Let it remind you to pray for all teachers in the land and in the world. They certainly need help for an effective job, and their reach of influence is enormous. The middle finger, being tallest, should remind you to pray for the very important people in the world, the leaders of nations. We are quick to criticize our political leaders, but what we ought to do is to pray down light and wisdom upon them. We should do so God said, "that we may lead a quiet and peaceable life in all godliness and honesty" (1 Tim. 2:1-3). The fourth finger is the weakest one, as every piano player knows. Let this finger remind you to pray for the weak, the heavy-laden, the burden-bearers, the sick, the anguished and the bereaved. Lastly, there is the little finger. This one should remind you to pray for yourself, for you are to be little in your own eyes." The patient did as the nurse suggested. Her outlook and attitude was transformed from negative to positive. In her own words, "What was formerly unbearable turned into a rich, rewarding experience, a wonderful blessing to me and, I am confident, to all others for whom I prayed."

GOD: I want your troubles to bring you gain. I do not want you to suffer and then have nothing to show for it.

MY RESOLUTION: When God decides that it is my turn to suffer sickness, I will try to make the best, not the worst, of the experience. I will think not only of what he is doing *to me* but also of what he is trying to do *for me*. I can't do much about the debit side, but I can do something about the credit side. Sickness is costly, but I know the price is right if the gain is great. I will not cry over the price if it helps me to gain the prize of everlasting life.

God's purpose in allowing pain is for our gain. When the pain is great, I can thank God that the gain is greater.

4.

Lord,
Now I
Understand

"Suffering trains us to endure" (Rom. 5:4 NEB).

When God allows us to suffer, he has his purpose. And a good purpose it is. He wants us to grow in our Christian life. The pain he allows is for the gain we need.

Paul understood the secret: "Our light affliction," he said, "worketh for us a far more exceeding and eternal weight of glory" (2 Cor. 4:17). Imagine that! "Affliction worketh for us." It's true! God is using afflictions to work on us for our good.

God Has to Do What He Does

God is the Competent Physician. His diagnosis of our condition is right. His knowledge of the therapy we need is perfect. He acts upon our need.

God said as much in his Word: "Now you smart for a little while, if need be, under trials of many kinds." He explains: "Even gold passes through the assayer's fire, and more precious than perishable gold is faith which has stood the test. These trials come so that your faith may prove itself worthy of all praise, glory, and honor when Jesus Christ is revealed" (1 Peter 1:6-7, NEB).

Three little words in this passage deserve emphasis. They are, *"if need be."* There is a divine *"if need be"* behind God's dealings with us. He never sends grief and pain because he delights in our misery. There is nothing whimsical, capricious, arbitrary, sadistic in God. He will take us into suffering only when we need it. For God's children there are no needless tears. Behind every trouble and tear there is a divine "if need be."

God has only our good in mind: "The God of all grace," says Peter, "will himself, after your brief suffering, restore, establish, and strengthen you on a firm foundation" (1 Peter 5:10 NEB).

God has to do what is best for his children.

If they need purification, he will get the oven ready. He has no choice, if he has their best interest at heart. And he does want their best. This should make them happy. "My brothers, whenever you have to face trials of many kinds," the Apostle James says, "count yourself supremely happy, in the knowledge that such testing of your faith breeds fortitude, and if you give fortitude full play you will go on to complete a balanced character that will fall short in nothing" (James 1:2-5 NEB).

The treasured ones are chastened. That truth prevails throughout the Word: "Blessed is the man whom thou chastenest, O Lord" (Psalm 94:12). "Happy is the man whom God correcteth" (Job 5:17). "Whom the Lord loveth he chasteneth, and scourgeth every son whom he receiveth" (Heb. 12:6).

Whom God Loves He Chastens

Christians expect God's disciplines. They know that God tests them, not to weaken them but to strengthen them. God's chastenings are intended to make us stand, not to make us fall. God wants to make us better, not bitter.

We should look upon God's chastenings as

an athlete looks upon his training. When his trainer intensifies the exercise, the athlete does not complain. He is training for triumph. Through strenuous effort he is getting ready to win the prize.

Suffering Yields Holiness

God calls: "Follow after holiness without which no man can see the Lord" (Heb. 12:14). Sin relates us to Satan, holiness relates us to God. God is working for our holiness. For holiness the Father sent his Son; for holiness the Son gave his life; for holiness the Holy Spirit is at work in us. God has one supreme purpose, "that we might be partakers of his holiness" (Heb. 12:10).

Holiness prospers most on the shadowed path. It was under persecutions that the church made its finest advances. Suffering weans us from sin. We don't feel like sinning when we are suffering. "When a man has endured bodily suffering," Simon Peter says, "he has finished with sin, that for the rest of his days on earth he may live, not for the things that men desire, but for what God wills" (1 Peter 4:1-3 NEB).

74

It is for holiness that God chastens us. In time of tribulation holy thoughts and holy desires well up in our hearts. Suffering is God's signet ring whereby his holiness is impressed upon us. That truth is illustrated in the parable of the wax and the seal.

"Unaccountable, this!" said the wax as from the flame it dropped melting upon the paper beneath.

"Do not grieve," said the paper, "I am sure it is all right."

"I was never in such agony!" exclaimed the wax, still dropping.

"It is not without a good design, and will end well," replied the paper.

The wax was unable to reply at once, and when it again looked up it bore a beautiful impression, the counterpart of the seal which had been applied to it.

"Ah, I understand now!" said the wax, no longer in suffering. "I was softened in order to receive this lovely, durable impress."

The Great Ones Suffered Most

See the noble army of sufferers! Abraham is tested. Joseph is afflicted. Moses is plagued.

David is persecuted. Job is harassed. Elijah is hated. Jeremiah is driven from home. Daniel is thrown to the lions. Stephen is stoned. Paul is imprisoned.

Suffering makes ready a people for the Lord. Most of the psalms were born in the wilderness. Many of the epistles were written in prison. The greatest hymn writers learned in suffering what they taught in song. We may thank Bedford jail for *Pilgrim's Progress*.

The soul struggles of Martin Luther brought on the Reformation. Asked how he could serve God so joyfully under stress, Luther replied: "That is what the cross has taught me."

We Gain Through Pain

If a man loses a dollar bill and in his search finds one hundred dollars his unhappiness in losing the lesser is offset by his joy in finding the greater. So it is with suffering and trouble. Whatever draws us closer to God, however painful or hard to bear at the moment, is a great blessing. Trials sweep away the debris that has cluttered life with things that hide God from our eyes. The shore is swept clean by the storm, and we get a new experience of the ocean of God's grace.

Through suffering our eyes are drawn from the glamour of sin to the glory of salvation.

Through suffering our ears become less attentive to earth's music and more attuned to the Hallelujah Chorus.

Through suffering our goals in life shift from earthly tinsel to heavenly treasure.

Through suffering our feet incline less to the inns of this world and more to the friendly and familiar road that leads home.

God's Strange Ways to Make Us Strong

God helps us in the strangest ways. He is for us even when it seems that he is against us.

We pray for peace, he gives us turmoil—that we may find our peace in him.

We pray for strength, he weakens—that we may find strength in him.

We pray for health, he lays us low—that we may find wholeness in him.

We ask for wealth, he gives us poverty—that he himself may be our riches.

We pray for joy, he gives us grief—that our joy may be in him alone.

There is an old story about a violin maker who searched all his life for wood from which to make violins of unusual beauty and power of tone. After long search he found the wood he was looking for, taken from trees at the timberline, the last stand of trees in the mountains. Here the winds blow so hard and steadily that the bark can barely grow. All the branches point one way and the trees are spread low above the ground. These trees produce the wood for the world's best violins.

Like those trees, God makes us strong through the hard and driving winds of adversity. We are brought to our knees, humble and helpless before him, but we're never broken or uprooted. We become instruments of beauty and power upon which God plays his music. The most exquisite music comes from the spirit sweetened through suffering, tempered through trial, purified through pain.

Perfection—Our Present and Ultimate Goal

Only two perfect men lived on this earth, Jesus and Adam. In Adam we lost the divine image. In Jesus we get it back.

The restored perfection of the divine image

—that is God's gift, and it has to be our goal. God wants us in fact to achieve what in faith we receive—perfection. "We wish even your perfection," said Paul (2 Cor. 13:9 NEB). Perfection is our constant ideal. No lower standard is admissible. The Christian ethic of behavior is this: "Be what you are!" You are holy in Christ. Now be holy in life. Strive to be as perfect in the eyes of men as you are in the eyes of God. You have the white robe of righteousness. Wear it proudly, keep it flawless, for every spot shows on it. "We are transfigured into his likeness, from splendor to splendor," Paul wrote (2 Cor. 3:18 NEB). There is only one true way: "Put on the new man, which after God is created in righteousness and true holiness" (Eph. 4:24).

Columbus had this daily entry in his logbook: "Today we sailed west, for that was our course." By charting his course and sticking to it he discovered a new world.

The daily course of life for the Christian on his way to the new world of perfection is to practice Christ likeness. Stay on that course, in his steps, and you'll reach the glory.

A little girl was watching a silversmith as he put the silver into the crucible over the fire.

As the flames grew hotter and hotter, the silver became a glowing liquid. The smith was bending over the liquid, watching it closely never lifting his head—not even to greet the visitor.

Finally the girl asked, "Why do you watch the silver so closely? What are you looking for?"

"I'm looking for my face," was the reply. "When I can see myself in the silver, then the work is done."

The heavenly Silversmith will keep us in the crucible of suffering until he sees his face.

5.

Lord,
Have It
Your Way

"It is the Lord, let him do what seemeth him good" (1 Sam. 4:18).

The highest compliment a person can pay God is to trust his love.

With full trust in God we accept his ways confidently. No more are we merely putting up with his chastenings, we are thankful for them. We may even go a step beyond that, and ask him to send us anything, however hard to bear, which he thinks good for us. This is a step of bold trust. Few dare it. But there are men and women of great faith who stand on such a high plateau of trust that they can say: "Lord, send me any trouble, any pain, and affliction, only grant that it may all work together for my salvation."

Edna Harridge exhibited such trust. When her doctor told her, "I have bad news for you," she said, "That's impossible—what God does has to be good news." Instead of the usual complaint, "Why is God doing this to me," Edna asked, "Why not? If he loves me as much as he says he does, then everything his fingers touch must turn into loveliness."

Our God Loves Us

In a meeting of world religious leaders in India the virtues of non-Christian religions were extolled. A Christian listened patiently. Then he rose to ask: "Do your gods love you?" The religious leaders answered: "Our gods do not know what love is." It was an open door for the Christian: "Herein I declare the supremacy of the Christian faith," he said. "Our God is love."

It is true. Our God loves us. The greatest demonstration of God's love for us has been his sending of his only Son into the world to give us life through him.

Reason cannot explain why God loves us as

he does. We are not as lovable as all that. But he does love us intensely. That is why he is always working for our improvement.

He cannot allow us to stay as we are. His purpose and goal for us is our progress toward perfection.

Everything in God's animate world must grow and be productive. That principle is written into creation. A tree that does not grow is dying. So is a person. Progress, development, growth is God's principle also in the spiritual world.

To ask God to be content with us as we are is to ask him to cease loving us. That is one thing he will not do.

The Christian Is a Divine Work of Art

Art and beauty, as well as science and nature, are an expression of the thought of God. But we, the redeemed, cherished children of God, are God's master-work. To have us as his own, God sent his Son into the world. His supreme purpose was to woo us back to himself. The dynamic of reconciliation was nothing less than the blood of the cross. In the death of his Son God is saying: "Now you know how much I love you. Enough to see my Son suffer and die for you." On the cross we can see our worth in the eyes of God.

Everything God does now should be interpreted in the light of what he has done at the cross. A father whose son was killed asked his Christian friend angrily: "Where was God when my son was killed?" The Christian answered: "He was exactly at the same place he was when his Son was killed."

"After you have suffered a while," God says, my goal and purpose is "to make you perfect." The Bible was written "that the man of God may be perfect" (2 Tim. 3:17). All activities in the church are "for the perfecting of the saints . . . till we all come . . . unto a perfect man, unto the measure and stature of the fulness of Christ" (Eph. 4:12-13).

God Is Sculpturing Us to Perfection

The heavenly Sculptor is at work moulding us into his beauty. He will not cease until his work of art assumes the character he wants. He may have to hurt us, but he will not injure us. If a block of granite could feel pain while the sculptor strikes with hammer and chisel, it would say: "Leave me alone. I want no more of this."

While God is chiseling away at us, we may wish that he had a less glorious goal in mind for us. But we really can't mean that. We know he is getting us ready for the galleries of heaven, there to appear in the very perfection of Christ.

Suffering Is Par for the Course

Suffering offers the best opportunity for amendment. Someone has said: "God whispers to us in our pleasures, speaks to us in our conscience, but shouts in our pain." Pain is God's megaphone to rouse us from deafness to his will.

God's children suffer not for the sake of suffering but for the benefit of suffering. What suffering does *for* them is more important than what it does *to* them. What it does to them is incidental and relatively unimportant.

There is more help in pain than most of us suppose. Pain is for gain. When we are sick, we ordinarily ask God to heal us or, short of that, to take us into heaven. That prayer is inadequate. We should also ask God to use the pain he allows for the gain he wants. God's purpose is to advance us in holiness, to achieve amendment of life, to beautify the spirit with the charisma that cross-bearing imparts.

A Luminous Paradox

"When I am weak," Paul said, "then I am strong." On the surface that sounds like nonsense. It is, in fact, profound truth.

When we understand this paradox we are ready to advance to the graduate level in God's School of Spiritual Advancement.

God told Paul, "My strength is made perfect in weakness." Paul understood what God meant. In his own case he discovered that a man may indeed be weak when he is strong and strong when he is weak.

The Apostle Simon Peter proved this paradox true. Jesus warned Peter and the other disciples to use prayer for reinforcement against Satan's attack. Peter disregarded the warning. He was strong enough for any emergency. He blew the test. He failed his Lord. What he said he would not do, he did; what he said he would do, he did not.

Peter's strength was his weakness, whereas Paul's weakness was his strength. Peter leaned totally on himself and lost. Paul leaned totally on Christ and won. Peter stood on quicksand. Paul stood on granite. Peter was too strong for his own good. The strength he counted on was his own. It failed him when the test came. Paul, recognizing his weakness, reached out for the strength of the Lord. This made him strong. "I can do all things through Christ who strengtheneth me," he shouted (Phil. 4:13).

All the great ones in God's hall of fame "turned their weakness into strength" (Heb. 11:34 NEB). God wants us to do the same.

Faith Brings Victory—Fear Brings Defeat

Most problems in life present the alternative of taking the way of faith or the way of fear. The way of faith is the way of victory, the way of fear is the way of defeat.

Small wonder that the fear issue is so prominent in God's Word. Fear is a greater enemy than we suspect. The first result of the first sin was fear. "I was afraid," Adam said when he encountered God after his defection. Sin brings fear.

The fear syndrome is present in each of us. And it has frightful results. It ravishes the mind, saps the body's strength, excites the emotions.

Fear is an enslaving tyrant. Thirty thousand people in London were afraid to go to work on the day their newspaper failed to publish the horoscope. "Fear hath torment," the Bible says (1 John 4:18). Experience proves that true.

For the torment of fear God offers us the comfort of faith. He wants us to live in faith, without fear. Someone has counted 365 "Fear nots" in the Bible. That is one for every day in the year.

Faith in God's love is the only way out of fear. "There is no room for fear in love; perfect love banishes fear," the Bible says. "Anyone who is afraid has not attained to love in its perfection" (John 4:18 NEB).

For the believer there is only one real fear, the fear of doubting God. Doubting God is bad business. "The doubter is like a heaving sea ruffled by the wind," James says, up one minute, down the next. He concludes, "A man of that kind must not expect the Lord to give him anything" (James 1:6-8 NEB).

A doubter said to his Christian friend, "I just can't come to the assurance of God's love." Wisely the Christian asked, "Whom are you doubting?"

Never Doubt God's Love

Only faith in the promises of a loving God can overcome fear. God does love us. That truth is the strongest overtone in the Bible. It is the central theme of Christianity.

God's love is there for us to claim, with no conditions attached. We don't have to put on airs to impress God, or agonize to achieve a level of holiness before we can be sure of his love. He loves us just as we are. In fact, we are precious in his sight. We are important to him. "A Christian," Martin Luther said, "is a child of God, a temple of the Holy Spirit, an heir of eternal life, a companion of the holy angels, a ruler of the world, a partaker of God's divine nature."

When we are sure of God's love, and God is sure of our trust, all will be well.

God's love and your trust—that's the winning combination. Never let a wedge of doubt come between these two.

In love the Captain of our salvation promises a safe landing. Trustfully we cling to that promise even though the waters roar and the storms rage.

Anchors That Hold in the Storm

God has put his promises in writing. Our security rests not on what we think or imagine but on what God said in his Word. "Man's word is a vapor of smoke," said Martin Luther, "but God's Word is a mountain of granite." We can put the full weight of our trust on the promises of the Word. God is faithful to his own promises.

The Chinese have a quaint and meaningful way of expressing the concept of faithfulness. They draw the symbol for man, and next to it the symbol for word. Faithfulness is a man standing by his word.

God is faithful. He stands by his Word. "I have loved you with an everlasting love," he declares; "therefore I have continued my faithfulness to you" (Jer. 31:3 RSV).

The man who stands or falls by the Word will never fall. Earthly values may crumble, but God's Word endures.

God's Light Is Brightest in Darkness

Three American POWs experienced the Word's power. One of them wrote: "Our cell was like a blackboard. On it with silver pencil

God wrote words of hope . . . words alive with light. We clung to them as a drowning man clings to a log. Everything was taken from us. Everything except God. We found him a very present help in trouble. This discovery of God made our imprisonment a most meaningful experience in life."

Their darkest night was the beginning of their brightest day. God brought them low to lift them high. He led them into the dark to bring them into the light.

God's Word is a power station. Those who plug their life into it will always have light and power. When it comes to power nothing can match God's Word and the Holy Spirit in the Word.

God still writes with silver pencil upon the blackboard of sorrow the promises of his Word. It is when life grows bitter that God's Word is sweet. "It is good for me that I have been afflicted," David writes, "before I was afflicted I went astray, but now have I kept thy Word" (Psalm 119:71,67).

Welcome, Dear and Holy Cross

"When all kinds of trials and temptations crowd into your life," St. James writes, "don't

93

resent them as intruders, but welcome them as friends" (James 1:2 Phillips).

When trouble knocks at the door of your life ask not, "Lord, what are you doing *to* me?" but, "Lord, what are you doing *for* me?" Ask not, "How *quickly* can I get out of this?" but "How *much* can I get out of it?" Ask not, "*How* can I get out of all this trouble?" but "*What* can I get out of it?"

Blind Eyes Sometimes See More

George Matheson, the renowned blind preacher of Scotland, learned how to welcome the cross as a friend. "My God," he wrote, "I have never thanked thee for my thorn. I have thanked thee a thousand times for my roses, but not once for my thorn. I have been looking forward to a world where I shall get compensation for my cross; but I never thought of my cross as itself a present glory. Teach me the glory of my cross; teach me the value of my thorn! Show me that I have climbed to thee by the path of pain. Show me that my tears have made my rainbows!"

Many cross-bearers would not exchange the cross for all the world's riches. A Christian woman in California lost her eyesight but, like George Matheson, gained 20-20 vision spiritually. "I praise God for my blindness," she wrote, "I now see more than ever before. My inner eyes have power to see the invisible things that are really permanent. God is closer to me than ever before."

The Victory of Faith

Lucille Cullimore returned home with a malignancy in the marrow of the bone. Doctors said it would be terminal. But God had other plans. Here is her story: "Family and friends came to my bedside. I was surrounded by love. All assured me of their prayers. I clung to the promise, 'The prayer of faith shall save the sick' (James 5:14). Hope was rising in my spirit, and I sensed strength entering my body. God was keeping his promise, 'They that wait upon the Lord shall renew their strength.' The earthly doctors did their best, but the heavenly Doctor did better. The most wonderful thing in my many hours of suffering was the gift of confidence and trust in God. I thank my fellow saints who bore me up on wings of prayer and placed me in the care of the Great Physician who healed me. Now, after eight years, I rise each morning thanking God for each new day."

Nothing Can Defeat Faith

Edith Dibble, a noble Christian saint, wife, and mother of four, departed this life in her prime years. Eloquently she gave proof of the power of Christian faith to rise in triumph above tears and pain, even the prospect of death. On her death bed she composed this poem:

Pity me not!
I'm in my Master's arms.
He holds me fast and will
Not let me go.

Welcome the thought
That Christ thus cares for me.
His good and gracious will
Is done indeed.

Alter in ought
My portion no hair's-breadth.
Remove no featherweight
Of burden light.

Cancel no jot,
The tittle he prescribes.
The Great Physician knows
What cure is best.

Weep now for nought
Since no iota, speck,
Of what the world calls trouble
Troubles me.

Envy my lot!
I'm in my Lord's embrace.
With such a Lover, who
Would sigh for change?

What hath God wrought?
This little season's pain
He blesses, turns into
Ecstatic joy!

Perfect the plot
My Heav'nly Bridegroom plans
Whereby he proves his love.
He kisses me!

To the believer help is only a prayer away. To the unbeliever it's a million miles from nowhere. The choice is ours: we can either go up by way of faith or down by way of unbelief.

God wants us to advance beyond the level of merely putting up with trouble. He wants us to make the best and most of it. That is what the oyster does when a bit of sand gets under its shell. The irritation is covered with a velvety substance which eventually becomes a pearl. A pearl is a victory over irritation. The testings of life are opportunities for pearl culture. God wants us to turn irritations into priceless pearls of Christian character.

Reach for God's Hand

When it is heavy upon us, God's hand is closest to us and within easy reach.

King George VI of England in a Christmas message had this famous quotation: "I said to a man who stood at the gate of the year: 'Give me a light that I may walk safely into the unknown.' He replied, 'Go out into the darkness and put your hand in the hand of God. That shall be to you better than a light and safer than a known way.'"

For every trouble God gives us a hand.

An elderly Scottish Christian who was ill was visited by his pastor. Seeing a chair drawn close to the bed, the pastor said, "I see you have had a visitor." "No," said the old Christian, "I keep the empty chair by my bed to remind me that Christ is there next to me. When I need help I reach out for his hand." That night the pastor had a telephone call from the daughter of the old Scot, telling of her father's sudden departure. "I didn't expect that to happen so soon," the pastor said. "Did he say anything before he died?" "No," said the daughter, "but I noticed one thing, he had his hand on the chair."

Live One Day at a Time

While suffering intensely Jesus remained strong, "knowing that he came from God and was going to God" (John 13:3 NEB). The pain of the moment was easier to bear when he thought of the glory of the future. We are on our way to God—that is the long dimension. Everyday is a day with him—that is the short dimension. Our now is with God, as well as our then. Today, tomorrow, and forever we are in God's hands.

A patient in the hospital asked her doctor, "Doctor, how long will I have to stay in bed?" "Just one day at a time," was the wise answer.

Instead of living one day at a time we are tempted to fret and stew about the future. It is foolish to bring the burdens of tomorrow into today. Our shoulders aren't strong enough to carry the burdens of more than one day at a time. Today is ours. Tomorrow may never come. If it does come, God will still be alive. He wants us to give to each day a heart of faith and courage. "Cast thy burden upon the Lord, and he shall sustain thee" (Psalm 55:22). That is his promise, and he will keep it.

Today may bring bitter tears, but he can kiss those tears into diamonds. All about us there may be gloom and pain, but with us there is a Friend who has never forsaken one of his own.

Today is ours to look at him in trust, to preach a living sermon of confidence in his promises.

The book of yesterday is closed; tomorrow's page has not been opened. Over yesterday God has placed the cloak of his forgiving mercy; over tomorrow he has written words of gracious promise. Yesterday's mercy and tomorrow's promise should inspire today's trust.

Let us then each day write the story of today. Let us dip our pen into the blue of God's love and write in the gold of his promises. Everyday like that has to be a good day. And days like that, strung together, merge at last into the day of eternal glory.

The Word Shows the Way

Do This:

Cast your burden on the Lord, and he will sustain you; he will never permit the righteous to be moved.

—Psalm 55:22

Believe This:

I have loved you with an everlasting love; therefore I have continued my faithfulness to you.

—Jer. 31:3 RSV

The eternal God is your dwelling place, and underneath are the everlasting arms.

—Deut. 33:27

Call upon me in the day of trouble; I will deliver you, and you shall glorify me.

—Psalm 50:15 RSV

HOLD ON:

We are afflicted in every way, but not crushed; perplexed, but not driven to despair; persecuted, but not forsaken; struck down, but not destroyed; always carrying in the body the death of Jesus, so that the life of Jesus may also be manifested in our bodies.

—2 Cor. 4:8-10 RSV

KNOW GOD'S PURPOSE:

Before I was afflicted I went astray; but now I keep thy word. . . . It is good for me that I was afflicted, that I might learn thy statutes. . . . I know O Lord, that thy judgments are right, and that in faithfulness thou hast afflicted me.

—Psalm 119:67, 71, 75 RSV

KEEP HOPE ALIVE:

For I am sure that neither death, nor life, nor angels, nor principalities, nor things present, nor things to come, nor powers, nor height, nor depth, nor anything else in all creation, will be able to separate us from the love of God in Christ Jesus our Lord.

—Rom. 8:38-39 RSV

We do not lose heart. Though our outer nature is wasting away, our inner nature is being renewed every day. For this slight momentary affliction is preparing for us an eternal weight of glory beyond all comparison, because we look not to the things that are seen but to the things that are unseen; for the things that are seen are transient, but the things that are unseen are eternal.

—2 Cor. 4:16-18 RSV

ACHIEVE GAIN:

A thorn was given me in the flesh, a messenger of Satan, to harass me, to keep me from being too elated. Three times I besought the Lord about this, that it should leave me; but he said to me, "My grace is sufficient for you, for my power is made perfect in weakness." I will all the more gladly boast of my weaknesses, that the power of Christ may rest upon me. For the sake of Christ, then, I am content with weaknesses, insults, hardships, persecutions, and calamities; for when I am weak, then I am strong.

—2 Cor. 12:7-10 RSV

Blessed by the God and Father of our Lord Jesus Christ! By his great mercy we have been born anew to a living hope through the resurrection of Jesus Christ from the dead, and to an inheritance which is imperishable, undefiled, and unfading, kept in heaven for you, who by God's power are guarded through faith for a salvation ready to be revealed in the last time. In this you rejoice, though now for a little while you may have to suffer various trials, so that the genuineness of your faith, more precious than gold which though perishable is tested by fire, may redound to praise and glory and honor at the revelation of Jesus Christ.

—1 Peter 1:3-7 RSV

We rejoice in our sufferings, knowing that suffering produces endurance, and endurance produces character, and character produces hope, and hope does not disappoint us, because God's love has been poured into our

hearts through the Holy Spirit which has
been given to us.

—Rom. 5:3-5 RSV

My son, do not regard lightly the discipline of the Lord, nor lose courage when
you are punished by him. For the Lord disciplines him whom he loves, and chastises
every son whom he receives. . . . For the
moment all discipline seems painful rather
than pleasant; later it yields the peaceful
fruit of righteousness to those who have
been trained by it.

—Hebrews 12:5-7, 11 RSV

COMFORT OTHERS:

Blessed by the God and Father of our
Lord Jesus Christ, the Father of mercies and
God of all comfort, who comforts us in all
our affliction, so that we may be able to comfort those who are in any affliction, with the
comfort with which we ourselves are com-
forted by God. For as we share abundantly
in Christ's sufferings, so through Christ we
share abundantly in comfort too.

—2 Cor. 1:3-5 RSV

Help Is Just a Prayer Away

Persist in prayer: "Will not God vindicate his chosen ones who cry out to him day and night, while he listens patiently to them?" Jesus asks. "I tell you," he affirms, "he will vindicate them soon enough" (Luke 18:7-8 NEB).

O Holy Spirit, give me the victory over doubt. I know that doubt grieves you and deprives me. When the storms rise and the shadows thicken, guard me against doubting your love, doubting your power, doubting your promises. Help me to believe that your love is true, your power is great, and your promises are trustworthy. I ask this in Jesus' name. Amen.

My dear God, I know Satan is mighty, but you are almighty. You have power to turn the tables on Satan. I pray, do this when he devises mischief against me. Turn to my benefit what he intends for evil. No matter how bad things are, keep me trusting your promise to make everything work together for good, through Jesus Christ my Lord. Amen.

O Holy Spirit, show me that suffering goes with the dignity and worth of life because it burns away the dross, develops trust in God's promises, and reinforces hope in the coming glory. Cultivate in me the noble and beautiful flowers that grow only in the shade. I ask this on the ground of Jesus' holy love. Amen.

Lord, in my nearsightedness I am always saying that the last thing I want is trouble, though it may be the first thing I need. If there were no trouble, I would perhaps get flabby in faith and flat in zeal. So I pray, let troubles come as your love and wisdom directs, but let my faith be so exercised and strengthened that I may rise to new heights of victory, through Jesus Christ my Lord. Amen.

O God, help me to be happy and cheerful at all times. When dark clouds move overhead, keep on reminding me that blue skies will come again. Give me the optimism based on the solid confidence that you are present and powerful in every situation. In Jesus' name. Amen.

Lord, teach me to respond faithfully to every cross you choose to lay upon me, lest I lose the intended blessing. Convince me that your chastenings are always loving, never punishing. Guide, direct, and uphold me that my crosses may be golden stepping stones toward the stars. I pray in Jesus' name. Amen.

O Holy Spirit, help me to be a willing learner in the school of tribulation. I want to be as faithful in learning the lesson as the heavenly Teacher is in teaching it. When I cannot understand all that is happening to me and around me, help me to trust. Give me power to believe the promise that all things must finally work together for the good of God's beloved and believing children. Amen.

My dear Lord, in good days help me to get ready for evil days. I want to stand steadfast in faith when the shock waves of trouble come. Teach me the high art of living always in your presence. Then, when fierce winds blow, give me anchors that will hold in the storm. I have nothing to fear when you are near. You told me so, and I believe it with all my heart. Amen.

O God, keep me in grace that I may never be more discouraged by what the world has come to than encouraged by what has come into the world through the Lord Jesus Christ. Instead of seeing only the wrong that sin has brought, help me to see all the right your grace has wrought. I ask this in Jesus' name. Amen.

O Holy Spirit, when I'm going through the dark valley of tribulation, keep on reminding me that cross-bearing and crown-wearing go together; that the love that chose us also chastens us; that the Lord who purchased us also purifies us; that the love that delivers us from death also disciplines us to life. In Jesus' name. Amen.

O Holy Spirit, give me victory over fear—the fear of failure, fear of sickness, fear of accidents, fear of bad news, fear of ridicule, fear of pain, fear of old age, fear of death. Fill me with faith in my Lord Jesus Christ who nailed to his cross every indictment against me and set me free from all evil. I pray this in his name. Amen.

O Holy Spirit, give me victory over pride— pride in my accomplishments, pride in my talents, pride in my possessions, pride in dress, pride of family, pride of intellect, pride of ability—knowing that all I have comes from you. Give me the victory of faith in your love, joy in your grace, contentment under your care, and zeal for your cause, through Jesus Christ, my Lord. Amen.

Lord Jesus Christ, free me from all anxiety —anxiety over yesterday's mistakes, anxiety over tomorrow's problems, anxiety over health, anxiety over things that may happen, anxiety over dear ones. Give me grace to place all my anxieties in your hands and to leave them there. I know your hands are good hands, strong hands, loving hands. Help me to trust them confidently. I pray this in your holy name. Amen.

O God, you have made it plain that I am strong when in my weakness I grasp your strength, and I am weak when I count on my strength. Lord, keep me leaning hard on your Word, trusting your promises, banking on your love, rejoicing in your grace. Then you will be the Source of my strength, my joy, my peace, my hope, through my Lord Jesus Christ. Amen.

My dear God, you have made it your responsibility to lead me to my goal and my responsibility to follow your leading. Your way, I know, is often hard, but always good. Help me to know that my safety consists not in the absence of danger, but in your presence. When you are near I need have no fear. Help me to remember that. I pray in Jesus' name. Amen.

Lord, when there is trouble, let my first thought be not how to get rid of it but how to grow by it. Lead me to ask how much I can get out of it, not how fast I can get away from it. Help me to look at trouble as the stuff to try the soul's strength on. Give me grace to turn stumbling blocks into stepping stones. I pray in Jesus' holy name. Amen.